Marijuana Stocks for Beginners

How to Invest in the Booming Pot Stock Market for a Big Profit

Alexander Bercovich

professional before attempting any techniques outlined in this book.

By reading this document, the reader agrees that under no circumstances is the author responsible for any losses, direct or indirect, that are incurred as a result of the use of the information contained within this document, including, but not limited to, errors, omissions, or inaccuracies.

Table of Contents

FREE BONUS

As a gift to you for purchasing my book I'm offering a special bonus - a free report relieving 3 Marijuana Penny Stocks with huge growth potential in 2020. These 3 Pot Stocks could be a big win for smart investors both in a short or long term.

Scan this QR code to get a Free Report

Introduction

Whether you support the legalization of marijuana or are against it, or you have your own stash of 420 in your sock drawer, one thing is for certain: the marijuana industry is growing.

According to Forbes (Dorbian, 2019), the industry is set to grow to become a $30 billion dollar industry by 2025. When someone uses a future date, it almost always seems far away. But 2025 is just 5 years down the pike. What's even more remarkable is the fact that the industry is currently valued at $17.7 billion. We are looking at a 69.49% increase in value within just 5 years.

Think about the fact that marijuana hasn't been completely legalized everywhere. And yet it is showing incredible growth.

Here's another fact. Researchers from the Colorado State University-Pueblo got together to check the impact of the marijuana industry in their county (Evans, 2019). They discovered that the popular plant brought the Pueblo County a little more than $58 million. They had a collected expenditure – that includes overheads, social services, and law enforcement – of $23 million, and if you deduce that from their gross gain, you are still left with a net profit of $35 million. That is still a cool profit for the county.

Especially considering that Pueblo County has fewer than 200,000 residents.

I believe that the growth of the marijuana industry is substantial. And it will create plenty of millionaires by the time we reach the year 2025. You can become part of the million dollar club as well. And the best part is that you don't have to come into contact with pot of any kind.

The trick is to be aware of the various companies that you can invest in and to have a specific investment strategy at your disposal.

You have to understand that the current projections of the marijuana industry are based on the present legal landscape. But as the landscape shifts, the projections are going to develop and improve. For example, there are 11 states that have legalized the recreational use of marijuana, while medical marijuana is legal in 33 states. What will happen if we add just two more states into the list of states who have legalized marijuana?

Ever since Canada became the first G7 country to make pot legal for personal use across the country, the repercussions of the country's decision can be felt around the world. Today, Israel has legalized pot for medical use. But in a recent 2020 update, the prime minister of the country, Benjamin Netanyahu, is considering following Canada's example and legalizing the plant for recreational use across the country. He has even created a special committee for the purpose.

Now I would like you to imagine the potential growth of the industry if Israel did implement the rule to legalize marijuana. A couple of states legalizing pot use can increase industry growth projections by a fairly big margin. What do you think will happen when an entire country does?

In 2018 Canada became the first of the G7 countries to make pot legal for personal use across the country. But the conversation around the legalization of marijuana has taken a dramatic shift. In the early 2000s, nearly 63% of the US population wanted pot usage to be illegal. By 2019, 67% of the US population wanted the country to take action (Geiger & Gramlich, 2019).

However, that 67% represents the part of the population who are in *favor* of legalization.

Within the past 20 years alone, there has been a drastic change in people's perspective. With the change in perspective comes an acceptance of the use of pot. According to one study made by Yahoo News and Marist University, more than half of American adults have tried marijuana at least

once in their lives. Nearly 55 million people –
which accounts for about a little over 16% of the
population – are "current users." In other words,
they have used marijuana at least once or twice
every year. Here is where things get even more
interesting. Over 40 million people are "regular"
users, who are people who use marijuana at least
once or twice every month.

Let's try and "zoom out" of one country. When we
examine the whole world, then we notice
something even more remarkable. The global pot
use has increased by 60% over the past decade,
with people smoking 130% more than before.
What this means is that as the global percentage
has seen a rise, so has the number of times each
person consumes pot.

I can give you plenty of other numbers, such as
the fact that when the state of Colorado first
legalized marijuana, customers shelled out $5
million for smoking pot and on cannabis edibles
such as candies, cookies, and brownies within the
first week of legalization. This increased the
yearly tax revenue of the state by $200 million, as
the week-on-week marijuana sales increased to
lead to a total annual sale of $1 billion.

I can also tell you that in Washington State, there
is a 37% excise tax on marijuana and all products
featuring marijuana. Once the state had legalized

pot, they saw a sudden boost in their tax revenues from pot consumption. All of the changes that you are witnessing right now is just the beginning. It is not just the US alone that is experiencing a paradigm shift, countries around the world are relaxing laws around marijuana use.

That shift is not merely important because it shows how accepting people can be about something, but it shows the huge potential for investors to make a nifty profit out of the marijuana markets.

Many skeptics have questioned the profitability of marijuana stocks and investments. They have many questions, but most of them revolve around the themes mentioned by the questions below.

If marijuana is so profitable, then why haven't many people considered investing in it?

The simple answer to that is they have! In 2017, cannabis stocks rose by 207.8% and continued to rise throughout the year. You might not realize this, but there are 16 pot-stocks listed in NASDAQ with a sizable value of over $15 billion. With recent trends, it seems like the stocks are showing a rise in their value.

Another reason is the apprehension people have when it comes to pot-stocks. Since the entire concept of marijuana stocks is still relatively novel, many people hold themselves back from investing in them because of perceived risks. They don't realize that currently, trading in marijuana stocks is like trading with any other industry stocks, only more rewarding.

Is the marijuana industry truly growing?

As we have just seen, it is. And might I also add that it is growing on a global scale. Since people are not informed about the statistics of the industry, they are unable to recognize the scope of the growth.

Think of the popular billion-dollar companies. Look at where they were and see the changes they have brought in the business landscape today.

Let's take a look at Amazon. When the company first opened for business in 1994, the situation was so dire that Jeff Bezos would go on to talk about how he would suffer from knee and back pains from packing all the items in stock.

When the company first went public in 1997, its stock was valued at $18 per share. That is not such a bad number, but it doesn't reflect optimism about the company's growth, especially after being 3 years in the market.

But as of February 16, 2020, the stock value of Amazon is an astounding $2,150 per share.

Experts believe that the price per share is only going to increase dramatically, with the price going up to as much as $5,000 per share by 2023.

Or let's take the example of Facebook. In an industry that was dominated by companies such as Friendster, MySpace, and Hi5, Facebook had it tough trying to get a proper market share. When it was finally opened to the general public in 2006, it did have a steady rise, eventually leading to its present value. As of February 25, 2020, Facebook's net worth is valued at $572.14 billion.

What I am trying to say is that both of the aforementioned companies had skeptics doubting their growth. They tried to do something that was fairly different.

I believe that history is repeating itself with marijuana stocks. We are already seeing substantial growth in the industry. The future is only going to show a massive improvement in the industry.

We have seen such growth in many industries that were once deemed dangerous to the public. Once the Prohibition period ended in 1933, alcohol markets boomed all over America. The situation is going to repeat itself, only this time, marijuana is going to be the product that is going to boom.

How can I make a profit through marijuana stocks?

Well, that is why I am here. I am going to guide you through the process and distill all the vital information you will require to get started on the stocks.

Chapter 1:
Overview of the Marijuana Industry

In the 1930s, a film to show the harmful effects of marijuana was released to the public. The film, titled *Reefer Madness*, was originally considered educational material. It was used by the public to raise awareness of the effects of marijuana. Eventually, as people began to change their attitudes about pot and with science releasing numerous research and studies based on cannabis, the movie turned into a piece of satire.

The above situation is especially true when science itself proved the medicinal benefits of marijuana. While it is still considered a controlled substance under federal government guidelines, it has come a long way from being included in the illicit drug category. Now, the stigma surrounding marijuana is changing at a breathtaking pace, and it won't be long before it becomes more widespread in the mainstream.

With its current status, numerous consumer cannabis product retailers and companies are already evolving to meet growing demands. One of the important reasons for such growth is that cannabis is not just restricted to bongs, pipes, or joints. There is a whole market dedicated to a variety of cannabis-based products, including topicals, infused products, and concentrates. Each product available in the market addresses the demands made by the modern consumer – that of ease of use, accurate dosing, and variety. Moreover, to meet the growing demands, companies and retailers are making use of unique advertising techniques and packaging. Cannabis products are not always handed over in simple baggies anymore. Manufacturers spend increasing amounts on the presentation of the product.

But I would like you to think about that for a second. Why would there be so much variety for a product that is not in high demand?

Products that are infused with cannabis often contain cannabinoids or other active components from the cannabis plant. Therefore, the products are fused with certain concentrates, allowing them to be sold on their own or, in some cases, as a combination with other products. For example, butter filled with cannabis can be sold on its own or as part of another product, such as cannabis cookies.

All of these innovations are significant because marijuana is now being used to cater to a huge market. A market that has its own tastes and preferences.

But to understand the market, we need to delve into it in more detail.

Market Highlights

CAGR

The cannabis market is forecasted to grow at a compound annual growth rate, or CAGR, of at least 32.6% from 2019 to 2026.

So what exactly is CAGR?

The term refers to the rate of return that is required to ensure that an investment is going to grow from its starting balance to a fixed balance in the future, also commonly referred to as the ending balance.

A CAGR represents the rate at which an investment rises if it had the same level of growth in the previous year, and the profits earned were reinvested at the end of every year until we reach the ending balance.

Let's see how CAGR works through an example.

Assume that you have $10,000 that you invested in a stock or any other market security.

Over the course of three years, your portfolio looks like the below:

- From January 1, 2015 to January 1, 2016, your portfolio grew to $14,000. This is an increase of 40%.

- From January 1, 2016 to January 1, 2017, your portfolio rose to $16,000, or an increase of 14.29%.

- From January 1, 2017 to January 1, 2018, your portfolio rose to $20,000, or an increase of 25%.

If an investor looks at the above numbers, then he or she might think that the increase in the second year was low, and it picked up by a small margin. However, it still hasn't risen above the first-year standards. He or she might become skeptical about market security and make future predictions based on his or her understanding of the market.

That's where CAGR comes in. It ignores the drastic changes between the years and focuses on the bigger picture.

It uses this formula:

CAGR = (Ending Balance/Beginning Balance)⅓ - 1.

When we plug in the values and convert it into percentage form, we realize there is a compound annual growth rate of 33.3%. This value helps investors understand what they can expect from the stocks in the future. For example, if they realize that 13% is a robust CAGR that gets them their return with a little profit, then anything above that is optimistic.

A robust CAGR for the marijuana industry is around 14.5%. However, as we had seen earlier, its actual CAGR is 32.6%, well above optimistic results.

Properties

One might ask: so what exactly is driving the cannabis market?

The pivotal factors that drive the cannabis market are the research studies conducted on marijuana, particularly those that have proven marijuana to have various medicinal properties.

It is for this reason that marijuana is more widely spread around the world for medicinal purposes. But the more it is used in the realm of medicine, the more doctors and health professionals have the opportunity to personally attest to its degree of harmlessness for recreational use. This, in turn, boosts the confidence of the government in legalizing marijuana. The countries that are currently using cannabis for medicinal purposes legally are:

- Australia
- Chile
- Colombia
- Germany
- Greece

- Israel
- Italy
- Peru
- Poland
- Portugal
- Uruguay

We are excluding countries such as Canada, the Netherlands, and the United States since all or many parts of the countries allow marijuana for recreational usage.

Dominant Market

The North American cannabis industry is set to dominate the market, mostly because of the fact that Canada had legalized the use of cannabis for recreational use in 2018, making it the first G7 country to do so. In the United States, with 33 states legalizing marijuana for medicinal use, the market has improved even more. Among the 33 states, Washington, California, and Colorado have the best-selling cannabis products in the entire country. This is an additional boost to the overall cannabis market since California also happens to be the most populated state in the US.

Major Developments in the Cannabis Industry

Here are some of the major developments that have happened in the cannabis industry in the past two years.

2018

In September of 2018, LATAM Holdings, a cannabis venture situated in Canada, was acquired by Aphria Inc. This move provides the acquiring company access to countries in the Caribbean and South America, such as Brazil, Jamaica, Argentina, and Columbia. The main aim is to show the government of the countries the profitability of cannabis, persuading them to enact better legalization laws in their respective countries. This will further increase the marijuana market, as South American and Caribbean countries have low cannabis market growth, as seen in the diagram below.

Cannabis Market· Growth Rate By Region, Global, 2018

High
Medium
Low

All the countries that have a darker shade, including South America, Africa, various countries in the Middle East, and other countries all have low cannabis market growth.

In October of 2018, Ontario Long Term Care Association, which is the largest association of long-term care providers in Canada teamed up with Spectrum Cannabis to find out how effective cannabis can act as a potential source of medicine for preventing the breakdown of cognitive functions. Could this be another milestone set by Canada that will improve worldwide perception about cannabis? Only time will tell.

2019

Demand for cannabis has encouraged companies to innovate even more. This has caused cannabis manufacturers to produce more value-added products, including oils, gels, and extracts. The whole phase of innovating products has been nicknamed "Cannabis 2.0" and is also marked by other additions, such as cannabis-infused vaporizers and beverages.

The growth of the cannabis industry can also be seen in smaller companies, which have moved up the value chain to become profitable prospects. Some of these smaller companies become attractive opportunities for bigger companies. For example, Verano Holdings was acquired by

Harvest Health for a little over $850 million, which is considered the biggest deal in the pot industry in 2019. Following the example of Harvest Health, Cresco Labs shelled out $825 million to acquire Origin House. The fact that even small-scale companies are valued at hundreds of millions of dollars might give you an idea of how big the cannabis industry has grown to become.

The Agriculture Improvement Act of 2018 in the United States has allowed for the production and distribution of hemp. Industrial hemp, which is simply referred to as hemp, is a variety of the cannabis plant. Hemp serves a wide variety of purposes, from proteins to fiber to smokable portions. They can be used to make building materials, furnishings, fabrics, clothing, and paper. While hemp and marijuana are both cannabis, their chemical makeup is entirely different. Marijuana, when smoked, can give the effect of getting "high," while hemp does not have the potency that marijuana does. However, the fact that it is now legal to grow hemp is a step further in the direction of progress.

Worldwide Trends

Because of the growing demand of cannabis around the world, the cultivation of the plant has increased. The data below shows that the cultivation of cannabis has not just increased compared to the last decade, but it is projected to increase even more in the next two years.

Worldwide Cultivation Demand (In Millions of Pounds)

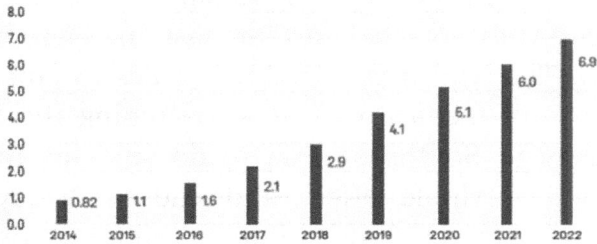

While countries in Latin America and Africa have shown low market growth, they have become ripe for investment. One of the main reasons is that global cannabis manufacturers are looking to reduce the cost of production. To them, the Latin American and African regions provide the resources that they require at lower costs. The situation is also improved because of many governments enacting new laws to support cannabis production. For example, the Ministry of Justice and Law in Columbia created a new committee in 2019 to respond to cannabis licensing requests within 30 days. The growth of requests for establishing retail and production units in the country has increased to a point that it was far better for the government to have a separate establishment to deal with the requests. Furthermore, the Colombian National Council of

Narcotic Drugs has increased the limit for cultivation. At 40.5 tons per year, they are aiming to meet the needs of as many cannabis producers as possible.

The "domino effect" of Canada's legalization process has traveled farther east. In December 2018, Thailand introduced new rules to approve the use of medical cannabis, becoming the first country in Southeast Asia to do so. This move created a ripple effect and caused Malaysia, Guam, Japan, South Korea, and even the Philippines – which is currently in the midst of a nationwide drug eradication effort – to legalize the use of cannabis for medicinal purposes. Certain provinces in China and India have also gained momentum for allowing the use of cannabis in medicine under certain guidelines. The important thing to note here is that if the major provinces of China and India manage to create better legalization laws, then the cannabis industry has access to a large market.

The Cannabis Industry Update for 2020

But why wait for the next two or five years to see the growth of the cannabis industry? You can see the growth the industry is experiencing in 2020 itself. Creating an investment strategy now will allow you to plan better for the future. Here are some of the major updates of the industry.

The US legal cannabis market had grown to over $13 billion in 2019, from $10 billion in the previous year. This year, the market is poised to grow to $17 billion. Those numbers show a 30.77% increase in growth this year, as compared to 30% growth in the last year.

Switzerland and Luxembourg are on the verge of legalizing cannabis this year. Both countries attract millions of tourists every year. The move to legalize cannabis will open the pot industry to a wider customer base. Mexico is also set to legalize cannabis by the end of April. If it does manage to pass legalization laws before the deadline, then it might be the third country in the world to allow the use of recreational marijuana.

Cannabidiol, or CBD as it is commonly known, is the second most prevalent component of a cannabis plant. While CBD is an important ingredient in medical marijuana, it is mainly derived from the hemp plant. We have seen how the US has legally allowed for the cultivation of the hemp plant. With that decision, the production of cannabidiol will steadily grow. This move is important because while many regions don't allow cannabis, they do allow products that are infused with cannabidiol, which range from food and beverages to makeup and skincare products.

The retail experience is going to improve this year, with a focus on "digital experience" to make retailers savvier. Customers can now have their preferences saved in the retailer database. So, the next time a customer visits the retail store, an update such as "Peter likes hybrid cookies" might already appear in the retailer's systems, allowing the store to keep the customer's purchase ready or update their existing purchases as necessary.

Market researchers are optimistic that the cannabis industry is going to grow by nearly twofold this year. You only have to look at the performance of Canopy Growth, the Ontario-based cannabis company and one of the largest manufacturers of cannabis products. Canopy Growth not only achieved a revenue of $96 million last year, which was a figure way ahead of industry estimates, but it also showed a 49% increase in sales over the previous year.

There were more than 9,300 active licenses for cannabis retailers and businesses in 2017, and the number is only showing growth. In 2020, that number is more than likely to cross the 10,000 mark, which is only going to improve the cannabis network.

Currently, many cannabis products are sold on the black market, owing to the lack of legalization procedures. However, if you take into consideration the entire market, then the market demand for cannabis is a jaw-dropping figure of $52.5 billion. This is one of the reasons why legalization procedures are gaining momentum; there is huge potential in the cannabis market. In fact, a fully legalized cannabis market can easily surpass the cigarette market, which is itself a $93.4 billion market.

When an industry grows, that industry provides better jobs in the market. Recent estimates of the marijuana industry have shown that the average salary per year that the industry offers is around $60,000. In 2018, the demand for jobs in the pot industry grew by 76%. In 2020, the growth is going to be even more significant because of the growth of the industry.

Chapter 2:
Are Weed Stocks a Safe Investment?

As an investor, you want to be sure that your money is flowing in the right direction. When it comes to up-and-coming industries, there is always a high degree of skepticism. For this reason, it is important to have a technical and fundamental analysis of the marijuana stocks to get a clear picture of your investment strategy.

Technical Analysis

Technical analysis is a form of trading evaluation discipline that is used to identify profitable trading opportunities by analyzing trends collected from trading activities and to evaluate investments that are already made. Technical analysis focuses on understanding the patterns behind trading signals and price movements. Using various charting software and tools to understand those patterns, investors are able to recognize the strengths and weaknesses of a security.

To use technical analysis, it is important to have the historical trading information of any security, whether that security is currencies, futures, stocks, commodities, fixed-incomes, or any other security.

You can perform technical analysis yourself by using one of the many tools available, but here are some important details about the cannabis market derived using technical analysis.

P/E Ratio of Major Weed Stock Companies

You utilize the price-to-earnings ratio, or P/E ratio, to measure the value of a company. It evaluates the latest share price of the company's stocks and compares it to its earnings per share (EPS). A company's earnings per share tells you the profitability of the company where the higher the EPS, the better profitability the company has.

When you connect a company's share price and its EPS, then you have a picture of how much value the company places on itself. For example, let us assume that a company has made above-average profits, based on its expenses and performance. Let us also assume that the company has a high share price. When investors evaluate the company, they notice that the share price is too high to justify the earnings per share. This means that the P/E ratio becomes high. When a P/E ratio is high, then it means that the company is overvalued. Investing in an overvalued company is risky because there is no record to show that the company has made enough profit to pay back the investors.

Let's take a simple example to illustrate the above point. Company A has made a profit of $10,000. They realize that they are going to increase their share price to $20 per share, and they currently have 1,000 shares in the market. With a profit of $10,000, they will only be able to return the investments of 500 people, assuming that each investor has only 1 share (1,000 shares = 1,000 investors). Therefore, $20 per share price overvalues the company and investors lose confidence.

There is no general consensus on what a good P/E ratio is. However, most market experts and investors agree that the lower the P/E ratio, the better the company's profile. Ideally, you should be looking at a P/E ratio that falls below 20.

One of the companies that have high profitability and low P/E ratio is Apple. The company has a forward P/E of 17.7. The company itself is profitable. It recorded a revenue of $265.6 billion in 2018.

But here is where things get interesting.

Did you know that there are marijuana stocks that have a lower P/E than Apple despite the faster growth that is projected year after year?

Let's first look at the three stocks that are showing incredible promise.

Trulieve Cannabis

P/E Ratio: 9.2

There is currently no marijuana stock that is cheaper than Trulieve Cannabis, which is a Florida-based company. The company has been able to make incredible profits, and the majority of the investors are optimistic about its growth. One of the major reasons for the growth of Trulieve's success is the fact that it mainly focuses on its home state of Florida. Despite the fact that marijuana can only be used for medicinal purposes in the state, it is the older population who are some of the major consumers of the plant. Currently, Trulieve has 30 stores in the state and has shown profits on a constant basis for quite some time.

Trulieve management has predicted total sales valued at $400 million for 2020, with most investors optimistic and confident about the company's predictions.

Valens GroWorks

P/E Ratio: 10.3

We had earlier discovered that there is an increase in cannabis-based derivatives, such as topicals, beverages, edibles, and various other products. The growth of such derivatives means that the demand for third-party hemp-extraction and cannabis providers is on the rise.

And Valens has positioned itself as such a provider really well. Valens provides a range of products, including cannabidiol, distillates, and even resins.

In 2019, the company signed a two-year contract with HEXO, a cannabis company, to supply them with 80,000 kilos of cannabis and hemp per year. It also signed another two-year contract for the supply of 60,000 kilos of cannabis and hemp per year.

Aphria Inc.

P/E Ratio: 12.08

Aphria has become the focus of many investors, mainly because of the fact that it had recently reported a revenue of over $79 million in a single quarter. It's annual capacity increased to 225,000 kilos as compared to 115,000 kilos production capacity the previous year. That's an incredible 95% increase in production capacity within a single year.

But its biggest accomplishment comes from the fact that when its year-on-year revenue growth was analyzed, the result is even more impressive. With a year-on-year growth of more than 500%, Aphria is easily one of the attractive marijuana stocks in the market today. However, Aphria still faces tough competition on its home ground from other major companies in the Canadian-based companies. We are going to examine these companies further into the book.

Village Farms International

P/E Ratio: 15.1

Village Farms has utilized a three-pronged approach to ensuring the profitability of the company stays high.

It's first approach is using its other business venture focused on growing vegetables. While the profit margin of the business is not too high, it does ensure a constant cash flow into the company, which the company then uses to fund its marijuana business. Additionally, the second business gives the company a fallback option.

The second advantage Village Farms has is its long-term contracts with various business entities. In 2019, the company had a peak production capacity of 150,000 kilos of cannabis and hemp. That capacity is set to grow this year.

Finally, Village Farms has also invested in planting hemp, securing over 720 acres of land for the purpose. This gives the company the essential raw materials it needs to keep its hemp production consistent.

Earnings Per Share

We have seen what earnings per share truly means. But if we are to use it as a yardstick to measure good stocks, then are there any that are promising?

There are. And you have plenty of stocks to choose from. Here are some options for you:

- Cronos Group (CRON)
- Canopy Growth (CGC)
- Tilray (TLRY)
- Aurora Cannabis (ACB)

- Aphria (APHA)
- CannTrust (CTST)
- Hexo (HEXO)
- Organigram (OGI)
- Sundial Growers (SNDL)

RoE

The return on equity (or RoE) indicates the financial performance of a company. It uses components such as shareholder's equity and net income to arrive at the result. In the world of investments, shareholder's equity is considered an asset to the company. Asset plays an important role in an RoE because it indicates how well a company is making use of its assets.

When looking at RoE alone, then the below companies stand out:

- Canopy Growth
- Cronos
- Aphria
- Aurora Cannabis

Charting

To check the performance of securities over a period of time, a chart gives you an accurate picture. Essentially, a chart is a graphical representation of the prices of securities within a predetermined time frame.

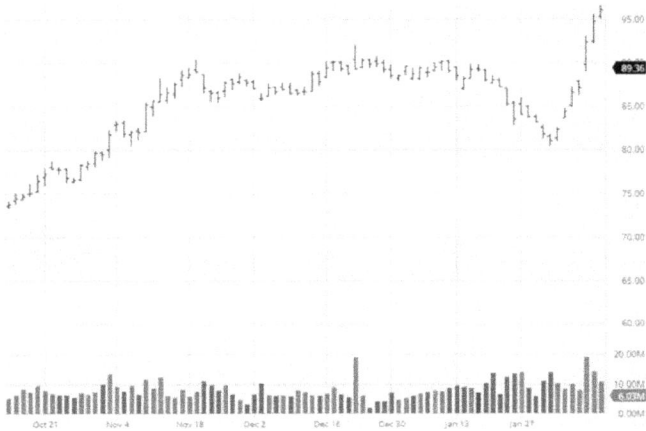

In the above example, we are looking at the performance of Abbvie Inc., a company that has been making waves recently in the marijuana industry. On the y-axis, you have the earnings presented in millions of dollars. Based on the latest report, the company has reached the $95 million mark in February 2020.

This progress is seen in not just one company, but across many companies across the industry.

In the above chart, you can see that there has been a steady growth month-on-month. However, the company showed a dip at the beginning of the year. This dip was caused by the outbreak of coronavirus at the beginning of the year. According to some experts (Williams,

2020), the cannabis industry depends on China for much of the equipment it requires, from lighting equipment to HVAC, that enables the proper growth of cannabis plants. With the recent outbreak and trade barriers, companies have to now turn to more expensive sources for their equipment. This unfortunate and rather unpredictable factor has caused a sudden uptick in costs over revenue.

However, recovery was fast for some companies such as Abbvie Inc. as they were able to bring back their stocks up.

Fundamental Analysis

Where technical analysis zooms in on the financial performance of the stock, a fundamental analysis looks at the stock from a broader perspective. It takes into consideration the financial and economic factors related to the company. For example, if you are using fundamental analysis on a pharmaceutical company, then you are also going to look at the drug laws of the country, where the company sources its ingredients, any risk factors, controversies, and other such news. The end goal is to use all the information to predict the direction of the company.

Let us examine the cannabis industry using fundamental analysis.

Revenue Growth

At this point, it is no surprise to know that cannabis is one of the hottest investment options. According to *The State of Legal Cannabis Markets – 7th Edition*, a special cannabis industry report prepared by BDS Analytics, the cannabis industry is set to grow into a $104 billion dollar revenue-earning industry by 2024. That number is truly high, no pun intended.

With the aforementioned growth prediction, it is also important to understand the legalization procedures happening around the world. When more countries in Europe begin to legalize marijuana, then Europe as a whole might surpass North America in revenue numbers. Before 2024, it is predicted that Europe might generate around $39 billion revenue while North America might contribute $37 billion in revenue. Additionally, the *The European Cannabis Report: 5th Edition* report (Prohibition Partners, 2019) shows that the use of marijuana in the medicinal field will outpace its use in recreational activities. This sudden shift in marijuana usage is actually quite favorable for the cannabis industry. The medical use of marijuana is gaining momentum. According to Harvard Health Publishing (Grinspoon, 2018), medical marijuana is known to treat chronic pain. While it cannot be used to manage severe forms of pain, such as those that arise from broken bones or post-surgery, it has been proven quite effective in managing chronic pain, especially those that are age-related, much better than opiates. Marijuana has also been known to manage the tremors in Parkinson's disease and act as a muscle relaxant. One of the most promising areas of research concerns the link between marijuana and PTSD management in war veterans who have been in combat zones. If a beneficial link can be discovered between marijuana and PTSD, then experts believe that cannabis can be used for treating stress and depression. If such potential benefits can be transformed into facts, then medicinal marijuana is going to get a massive boost.

SWOT Analysis

A good way to understand any industry is to have a SWOT analysis of it. SWOT stands for Strengths, Weaknesses, Opportunities, Threats.

Cannabis Industry: Strengths

The cannabis industry is on an upward trajectory of growth.

This is in stark contrast to the situation a few years ago, when even the word "cannabis" could not be spoken out in public. If people sold it, they would not mention it. If people consumed it, they would do it in private. Pot, weed, and marijuana were phrases one did not use in a normal conversation. It almost felt taboo, as though people were tip-toeing around the topic of cannabis, too afraid to broach it for fear of repercussions.

Today, the situation is entirely different. However, the benefits of legalization are not spread out equally. Some areas enjoy more benefits than others. For example, California is the biggest pot market in the United States. But even though not all states have legalized marijuana, the ones that have created a booming market for jobs. From cashiers to shop owners, jobs have been on the rise. When an industry starts providing job opportunities, it is an industry that the public wants in the community. Already, the public is showing its support for the cannabis industry. According to Pew Research Center (Daniller, 2019), the percentage of adults who were opposed to the cannabis industry has dropped from over 52% in 2010 to just 32%. This means that nearly two-thirds of the American public are in favor of legalizing marijuana.

Earlier, we saw the potential of marijuana in the medical field, which could further strengthen its stance in the eyes of the public and for policymakers.

Cannabis Industry: Weakness

While the conversation surrounding marijuana is improving, it is still not fast enough. The cannabis industry still finds itself in the gray area. There are still people who are skeptical about the plant and its properties, despite science backing up the claims.

I suppose this is partly because of fear. There are many who are worried about the repercussions of allowing the public use of marijuana.

Additionally, since cannabis is still not legal for sale or consumption in many places, business owners suffer. They don't receive the same tax deductions that other businesses receive. Banks and other financial institutions are apprehensive about offering loans, providing financial support, or even offering financial management services. These financial institutions fear potential regulatory and legal repercussions.

But this problem does not merely extend to banks and financial institutions. Venture Capitalists (VCs) are holding themselves back from placing their investments in cannabis businesses. It does not matter what the statistics or numbers say; they are more concerned about the legal nature of providing support to marijuana businesses. They still think that the future of the industry is somewhere in the gray area.

The situation makes things difficult for businesses. If the banks are unwilling to help, and VCs are refusing to provide the necessary cash flow, then cannabis businesses suffer from getting things off the ground. While the numbers look good in the stock market, the banks and VCs believe that there isn't enough compelling evidence for the marijuana industry to look good on paper.

Cannabis Industry: Opportunities

The advantageous part about the cannabis industry is that it is its own opportunity. From the moment Canada legalized marijuana, the world began to see cannabis in a different light. The industry is fresh, and despite the slow growth, it is still moving in the right direction. You might not think this possible, but just go online, and you are going to be surprised to notice the number of job vacancies in the cannabis industry.

But the opportunity lies not just for the people, but for the government as well. Case in point, Canada. When the country legalized marijuana, they wanted to curb down on illegal distribution as well. Hence, many provinces created official websites that sold the plant and its many products. These websites were the legal way to get hold of marijuana.

Through the website, the government could ensure that the products were of the highest quality and without any impurities. In other words, the product is safe for purchase and usage.

And guess what happened?

Within just 24 hours, all the websites ran out of marijuana.

The results were so unexpected that the government was not prepared to restock the website so quickly.

The marijuana industry is a giant opportunity, both for the public and the government. When the government realizes that when it begins to create a source for cannabis supply, then it is only going to open up new revenue streams. And if the situation is Canada is anything to go by, then a cannabis supply is a highly profitable one.

Cannabis Industry: Threats

There are two major threats to the industry, and after reading about the cannabis industry, you might be able to guess at least one of them. If you guessed the slow pace of legalization, then you are right.

Regulations are still a major threat to the cannabis industry. Not only can the industry not secure proper financial support, but it is unable to reach out to customers efficiently. Because only a few places have legalized cannabis, the usage and distribution regulations surrounding marijuana are not clearly defined. Furthermore, usage limits and restrictions are slowly getting more lenient.

Additionally, law enforcement is also concerned about cannabis usage, since there is no method to check the marijuana levels in a person's body. This situation causes a further push against the leniency placed on distribution and usage.

The second threat that the cannabis industry faces is supply. The demand for the product is high, but if we are to learn anything from the situation in Canada, then we know that stock can disappear as soon as they arrive in the inventory. Because of current restrictions, there isn't enough quantity produced by companies and suppliers to accommodate the demands of the government. Each supplier produces just enough to meet the demands of his or her customer. If they produce too much, with the government still unsure about its legalization procedures, then they might be left with a large stock and small customer base, thereby reducing their margins.

Beta

Beta measures the degree of volatility of a stock or security. It can also be used to measure how sensitive and elastic an asset is in the market. Understanding beta allows you to examine the risks involved in your investments better.

Because cannabis is such a hot product, it is going to go through what is commonly referred to as "growing pains," which are challenges and drastic price shifts that are going to put every investor on edge. Let's not forget the regulations that are still in place in the cannabis industry, and it's still an uphill battle for the industry.

For many cannabis companies, the stock market prices can be more volatile than the benchmark established by S&P 500. The S&P 500 is a stock market index that focuses on the market performance of 500 large companies in the United States. The fact that cannabis companies have made it into the S&P 500 is in itself a big deal. But that is merely a small victory in a battle that is long and full of challenges.

So how does one use a beta?

If a stock has a beta that shows 1, then it has the same level of volatility as the market. This means that the stock is not too risky, but it is not too safe either. If the beta is 0.5, then the stock has half the volatility of the market, and consequently, if the beta is 2, then the stock has twice the volatility of the market.

While the volatility of cannabis is fairly high, it is the position of the top three cannabis companies that has everyone's attention. These companies all have betas that are 260% more volatile than the market standards.

Let's look at some of these companies.

Hexo

While Hexo's stock prices have quadrupled in the last three years, it still faces a high market volatility. For example, its stock price boosted up to $8 per share in April of 2019 but dipped down to just $2 by just the middle of October. It then rose back up again at the beginning of 2020, but this level of market volatility often keeps investors from making bold decisions with the stock.

Current Beta of Hexo: 4.68

CannTrust Holdings

The surprising thing about CannTrust Holdings is that its production capacity peaked at 300,000 kilos in the year of 2019. That is enough to erase the skepticism of even the most doubtful investors in the market. But once again, production capacity alone is not going to convince anyone. Remember what we said about fundamental analysis? Investors look at the market scenario as a whole, including economic shifts, decisions of lawmakers, and other such components. While the legalization process of the cannabis industry is growing slowly, it is still a growth that doesn't place much confidence in the eyes of investors.

Current Beta of CannTrust Holdings: 4.45

Canopy Growth

If you are entering the stock market for cannabis, chances are that Canopy Growth will catch your eye. The company has become a hot commodity in recent years and has finally evolved to become the largest pot stock in the world in terms of market cap.

However, despite its big presence, it does not mean it is completely immune to the effects of market volatility. With a production capacity of 500,000 kilos last year, it has easily become Canada's second largest weed producer. However, the problem with the company lies in management decisions. With the former CEO, Bruce Linton, fired from the company and Mark Zekulin, the present CEO only acting as a stand-in until the company finds a replacement, the situation only makes investors feel as though the company does not have any long-term plan for itself. It is important to realize that changes happen in every company. People leave the company, even CEOs. However, when the cannabis situation isn't stable, any changes in management only worsens the situation for a company.

Current Beta of Canopy Growth: 3.67

Dividends

A dividends refers to the percentage of earnings that is distributed to its shareholders as reward. The amount of dividends that a company pays back to its shareholders depends on company revenues and the decision of the board of directors. Dividends can be paid as stock shares, cash payments, or any other form of property. But one thing is clear: the ability of a company to distribute dividends reflects its progress.

When most investors are evaluating marijuana stocks, the last thing that comes to their minds is dividends. This is because the cannabis industry is still really young when compared to other industries. Any new company being listed utilizes the money they receive for expansion purposes. They do not have much capital remaining to provide as dividends.

Now, that does not make them poor investments. After all, dividends alone do not indicate a company's performance. Remember that dividends are paid out depending on the board's decision. So, you might have invested in a popular tech company that is showing incredible profits over the last few years, but that does not mean you are going to receive a large dividend.

When it comes to the marijuana industry, investors make money through other means, such as capital appreciation, which indicates a rise in stock price.

But despite the situation, there are companies that are able to provide dividends. Below is a list of companies, and their dividend yields as of 2019.

- AbbVie Inc.: 5.67%

- Associated British Foods Plc.: 1.67%

- Aurora Cannabis Inc.: 1%

- Compass Diversified Holdings Inc.: 6.06%

- Innovative Industrial Properties Inc.: 4.25%

As mentioned earlier, do not use dividends to choose your stock. You need to evaluate the company's financial progress and market sentiments as well.

However, the fact that many companies are already capable of providing dividends to their shareholders shows just how much the industry is growing. Within just the next few years, the growth of the industry might drastically change companies' policies toward shareholders.

Getting High on Stocks

While it might seem tempting to look at dividends of a company, and then create investments plans accordingly, remember to collect the entire picture. To get the entire picture, you should look at past data as well.

Chapter 3:
Investment Opportunities in Marijuana Stocks in 2020

Before the legalization of marijuana in 2018, there was an industry that was still profitable.

Despite many rules and prohibitions around the world, the cannabis industry earned around $7 billion in global sales. You have to understand that the majority of the transactions were not made out in the open.

You might think that the restrictions might lower the profitability of the industry. But that was not the case. In 2017, the cannabis industry increased its revenue figures to $9.5 billion.

In 2018, the revenue grew even larger. Long before legalization laws were introduced in Canada, the industry was already on the rise. By the end of 2018, the industry had made a global revenue of $12.5 billion.

Anyone who had invested in pot stocks in 2016 would have at least made a cool million by now, mainly because of the fact there weren't many investors back then and the opportunity was ripe to make a lot of cash.

Let us look at companies who have grown immensely since the introduction of legalization laws.

Auxly Cannabis Group

Among the many new pot stocks that have arrived in the market, Auxly Cannabis Group probably ranks among the fastest growing stocks. In the beginning of the year, the stock value was priced at $0.70 per share at the beginning of 2019.

Since then, the company has shown a massive increase in sales by 1,109%. So you can only imagine just how much the share prices have grown recently.

This progress also allowed the company's share price increase from $0.61 to $0.75 within the year.

Flowr Corp

Another company to keep an eye out for is Flowr Corp. At the beginning of 2019, the company recorded total sales of nearly $10 million.

At the beginning of 2020, that number had rocketed up to $80 million. That's a growth of nearly 700% in sales.

This massive boost in sales increased the share price from $2.47 per share to a peak of $5.49 well before the middle of 2019.

The Green Organic Dutchman

With a fancy name like The Green Organic Dutchman, the company has also ensured its sales have been fancy across 2019. It had enjoyed a sales growth of more than 540%. In 2019, it had a production capacity of 219,000 kilos. But because of its growth, the company is planning to increase its production capacity to around 20,000 per month to 22,000 per month.

The growth of the company also boosted its share value, going from just $1.81 per share at the beginning of 2019 to reaching $3.62 even before the month of March had come to an end.

Cresco Labs

The growth of Cresco Labs is something that took the markets by storm. At the beginning of 2019, the sales of the company settled at $132 million. But at the beginning of January, the sales had taken a massive leap, ending at $545 million. That's an incredible 312% increase, and while that percentage increase might not sound as impressive as the ones made by other companies on this list, let's not forget the sales numbers.

The share price numbers also showed a massive increase. It went from $5.15 at the beginning of 2019 to $13.21 by the time it was May.

The Valens Company

The Valens Company showed an increase of nearly 210% in 2019, allowing it to catapult its sales to $131 million by the end of the year. If the trend continues, and the company meets its deadlines this year, then it will officially increase its production capacity to 1 million kilos by the beginning of next year, which is a huge step in meeting the growing demands of the public.

Share prices of Valens went from a mere $0.89 at the beginning of 2019 to $3.43 before the month of June.

Opportunities in 2020

To understand market opportunities, we need to understand the concepts of bull and bear market (and exactly why they are called that).

Bull and bear markets are terms that are used to describe the performance of the stock market. The terms highlight whether the market is appreciating or depreciating in value. Additionally, since the markets often reflect the sentiments of the investors and react accordingly, the terms show whether investors are optimistic or pessimistic about the market.

A bull market shows market conditions that are on the rise. It is denoted by a rise in share prices and investors are more confident about the upward trajectory of the conditions. When the market is on the rise, then the industry's economy is strong and employment opportunities are high. This is why the employment condition of an industry explains the position of that industry. For example, if you have invested in the oil industry because of how much profits you have noticed recently and all the wonderful projections made by experts, you still need to look at other factors. If you notice a widespread loss of jobs in the industry, then you know that the market is going to take a dip in the near future. People leave jobs all the time. However, that shouldn't indicate that the job positions themselves are disappearing instead of becoming vacant for fresh talent or labor. A big exodus of the workforce spells disaster to the industry. Rising markets are called bulls because of the way the animal attacks. A bull raises its head, moving upwards to strike.

A bear market is the opposite of a bull market. The market is in decline, share prices are dropping, and investors predict a negative outcome. The economy of the industry slows down in a bear market and job opportunities decrease or companies start downsizing. A market is termed bear because of how the animal attacks; it swipes down with its claws when aggressive.

Now that we have gotten that primer out of the way, let's examine the cannabis market.

It is no secret right now that the cannabis industry faced numerous challenges in 2019. But this year, the market is looking increasingly bullish. Here are some indicators that show why the market might go for a drastic upward trend.

Legal Cannabis Spending Worldwide Forecast (US$ billions)

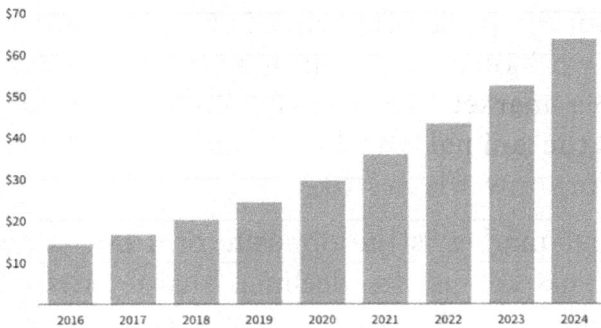

Growth of Companies

This is because of many changes happening across the industry. So far, Canada is leading the cannabis industry because of Canopy Growth, which is the largest cannabis company in the world presently. But in 2020, there is much growth occurring down south in the US as companies such as Trulieve, Curaleaf, and Green Thumb Industries rise up to take up profitable positions in the market. When new companies are able to show success and growth in the industry quickly, then it is a sign of an upward trend.

Increased Legalization

Another change that you will see in 2020 is more states legalizing cannabis. At the beginning of 2020, the Governor of New York, Andrew

Cuomo, was vocal about cannabis legalization and that the process was high on his list of agendas. A ballot initiative has been implemented in New Jersey, which will legalize recreational use in November. Another state where it is highly likely that legalization will take place is New Jersey. This is a huge opportunity for the cannabis industry, especially considering that Florida is the third most populated state in the county, followed by New York. Many legislative initiatives have already been set in place to legalize recreational use in Arizona, Minnesota, New Mexico, North Dakota, Connecticut, Missouri, Nebraska, and Oklahoma.

Agency Groundwork

In December 2018, the Farm Bill was introduced by President Donald Trump. This bill allowed for hemp production in the country. However, since then, there has been a lack of support from the Food and Drug Administration (FDA) and Drug Enforcement Administration (DEA). However things are going to change this year, since both agencies are going to lay down the groundwork for how the plant should be produced, manufactured, marketed, and sold. Groundwork is important because it will allow potential cannabis businesses to understand how to operate confidently. No more will these businesses have to operate on assumptions. They can confidently distribute cannabis under specific guidelines.

International Opportunities

For quite some time, the German market has been considered a profitable market for medicinal marijuana. This is not just because of its population, which is close to 70 million people, but the fact that marijuana-based medicines are fully approved in the national health system. Companies are already looking to invest big in the German market.

New Zealand has already introduced a binding referendum that will legalize marijuana for recreational use among adults. It might even beat Mexico's deadline for legalization, and if so, then New Zealand might become the 4th country to legalize cannabis.

ETFs and What You Should Know about Them

One of the oft-repeated phrases of the securities market is ETF. But what exactly is it, and why is it important for marijuana stocks?

Simply put, an exchange-traded fund is a type of security that includes a large number of stocks and securities. In other words, marijuana ETFs offer you a collection of marijuana stocks to trade with in a particular market.

Let's take a look at some of the prominent ETFs in the market today. Do note that the below numbers were based on February 2020 standings.

ETF Name	Symbol	Total Assets (in millions of US dollars)	Asset Class
ETFMG Alternative Harvest ETF	MJ	$629.83	Equity
AdvisorShares Pure Cannabis ETF	YOLO	$40.08	Equity
Indxx MicroSectors Cannabis ETN	MJJ	$27.68	Equity
Cannabis ETF	THCX	$18.86	Equity
AdvisorShares Vice ETF	ACT	$10.30	Equity
Cambria Cannabis ETF	TOKE	$9.35	Equity
Indxx MicroSectors Cannabis 2X Leveraged ETN	MJO	$8.37	Equity
Global X Cannabis ETF	POTX	$8.14	Equity

The Pros and Cons of Investing in ETFs

As with any security, ETFs also have a list of pros and cons that you should be aware of.

Pros

- ETFs offer the opportunity to diversify your portfolio. When you are investing in a number of stocks, then you are not depending on a single company or entity for your returns.

- They are much easier to trade, also because of the many securities you trade in at the same time.

- The expense ratios of ETFs are lower than many other securities.

- Many ETFs offer you dividend yields.

Cons

- Because of diversification capabilities of securities, the commission structures are usually high, chipping away your profit margins.

- There is a chance that the tax on ETFs can be higher than dealing with a single security.

65

Chapter 4:
The Boost of the Marijuana Industry in 2020 and Beyond

We have looked at some of the changes that will take place in the cannabis industry. It is time to look at exactly why the industry will grow in 2020, and beyond.

Why Will the Marijuana Industry Sky-Rocket in the Coming Years?

Benefits to the Economy

Pretty soon, politicians won't be able to ignore the potential economic contributions of the marijuana industry. The industry is already set to blow up into a $57 billion industry without all the states legalizing marijuana. Additionally, experts believe that with the present situation – having only a select number of states that have legalized marijuana – the industry is set to become a $41 billion industry by 2025. Imagine if all states decided to legalize marijuana. The numbers are going to be staggering.

Public Reach

At one point, even talking about using marijuana was filled with concern. Fast forward to 2019, and there are legal dispensaries in strip malls. Jobs in the cannabis industry are being posted publicly in online domains. Such changes are occurring all over the country, and the more they happen, the more the government has to pay attention.

Spread of Hemp

The Farm Bill was just the beginning. When it was launched, many anxious farmers breathed a sigh of relief. This is because they often find themselves facing tariffs when growing hemp. With hemp creating a lucrative industry, especially in the form of cannabidiol, it won't be long before hemp becomes a household name.

New Pot Stocks

Curaleaf Holdings. Neptune Wellness Solutions. Innovative Industrial Properties. These are just some of the companies that are going to show growth in 2020. Curaleaf alone is set to become a pot stock that might reach $1 billion in sales within the next two years. When such massive projections are revealed, banks and other financial institutions won't be able to ignore the potential. When more companies begin to show profits, the financial institutions and VCs will become more confident in investing in the cannabis industry.

Spread of Recreational Use

The below numbers show the revenue growth in Colorado, where marijuana has been legalized for medicinal use.

Calendar Year	Revenue By Calendar Year	Total Revenue Since Feb 2014
2014 (Feb - Dec)	$67.594.323	$67.594.323
2015	$130.411.173	$198.005.496
2016	$193.604.810	$391.610.306
2017	$247.368.473	$638.978.779
2018	$266.529.637	$905.508.416
2019 (Jan - Mar)	$63.490.118	$968.998.534

With such numbers being recorded, other states will soon understand the potential of the marijuana industry. This will compel them to allow marijuana for recreational use. When that happens, the growth of the industry will truly skyrocket.

15 Pot Stocks that Are Promising

1: Cronos Group

Stock Symbol: CRON (Nasdaq)

With competition rising, Cronos Group has somehow managed to stay at the front of the pack, coming out as an unofficial leader. Recently, Cronos became the target of a successful acquisition by one of the world's largest producers of tobacco, Altria. This means the company is able to enjoy a large influx of capital, making it a promising stock to look out for.

Cronos has itself acquired Redwood Holding Group, giving it access to the large cannabidiol market in the U.S.

2: Aurora Cannabis

Stock Symbol: ACB (NYSE)

Aurora Cannabis was large in the illegal market. However, when it entered the public eye, you would think that it would have a tough start owing to its history. The opposite was true. Aurora's reputation was so good that it picked up strong after going legal. If the conditions of the local Canadian and international markets improve, then Aurora's stocks could reach new heights.

3: Canopy Growth

Stock Symbol: CGC (NYSE)

One of the reasons why CGC is considered a darling of Wall Street is because of the fact that it is aggressively expanding into new territories. The company realizes that they have an incredible opportunity to take advantage of if they move fast. However, the only thing standing in the way of their progress is the lack of progress in legalization laws.

Constellation Brands, a Fortune 500 company and manufacturer of spirits, wine, and beer has also acquired 40% of Canopy Growth, giving the cannabis company a huge boost in capital. Despite the change in CEO, the company has exceeded expectations in the fiscal third-quarter report in 2019.

4: Tilray

Stock Symbol: TLRY (NASDAQ)

While Tilray started strong, it began to show a decline in the previous year. It opened at an incredible $70 per share at the beginning of the year but showed a bearish performance. Eventually, stock prices plummeted by more than 70% by the end of the year.

However, market experts are looking at the company with optimism, mostly because of international interest in Tilray rising. If you are averse to risk, then you might not want to go for Tilray. But if you are tolerant of risk, then you should know that if the company grows, then the payoff is going to be huge.

5: Aphria

Stock Symbol: APHA (NASDAQ)

Earlier, we discussed just how high Aphria's P/E ratio is currently. Now, we are going to talk about its consistency. There is one thing that investors enjoy about companies: their degree of consistency. This does not mean that companies do not experience lows. Rather, it means that the company keeps on improving despite the lows. APHA has always been a profitable company, and if new laws come into place, then it could boost the company's standing.

6: GW Pharmaceuticals

Stock Symbol: GWPH (NASDAQ)

Here's the surprising fact about GW Pharmaceuticals; it is a biotech company. However, it became extremely profitable after releasing its flagship product, Epidiolex. The drug is infused with cannabidiol and is used in therapy for seizure treatment and management.

Technically, you cannot look at GW Pharmaceuticals as a cannabis company, but it has gained tremendous profit from a cannabis-based drug. And that is why investors often consider the company when choosing pot stocks.

7: Curaleaf Holdings

Stock Symbol: CURLF (OTC Markets Group)

There has been much turmoil in share prices of Curaleaf in the first half of 2019. Investors almost felt like they were on a rollercoaster ride, and they had no idea how it would end. Fortunately for the company, the ups and downs ended on a high note. Curaleaf's stock had increased its value by 35% during November of 2019. Ever since then, there has been an upward trajectory in its progress.

8: Green Thumb Industries

Stock Symbol: GTBIF (OTC Markets Group)

Even though Canada is still leading the marijuana market share race, it does not mean that US companies are simply staying put. The company's stocks showed a bullish nature during the first quarter of 2019. Ever since then, the stock value has risen by 41%. One of the benefits that Green Thumb enjoys is its range of branded products. The company has proven that brand identity can indeed attract a large customer base.

9: Harvest Health & Recreation

Stock Symbol: HRVSF (OTC Markets Group)

Harvest's main source of profit lies in the medicinal marijuana sector. While it does offer recreational products, it is the medical sector that is the biggest contributor to the company's revenue. Recently, Harvest has also expanded its consumable, ointments, and oils range. This could help improve its stock prices in 2020.

10: Innovative Industrial Properties

Stock Symbol: IIPR (NYSE)

Innovative has the distinction of being the first ever marijuana company to be listed on a major stock exchange. Ever since then, the company has kept a steady growth. In 2019, its stock value rose by 39%. For 2020, investors are optimistic that it will produce the same result as the previous year, if not better.

11: Hexo

Stock Symbol: HEXO (NYSE)

Hexo is a slightly controversial stock. It has proven to be highly unpredictable in 2019 and even in 2018.

However, the company has recently invested big in its products, especially in the areas of edibles and beverages infused with cannabidiol. This could be a move to take advantage of the legalization changes occurring all over the world. If it succeeds, then the company could enjoy high returns. And so will its investors.

12: Acreage Holdings

Stock Symbol: ACRGF (OTC Markets Group)

Acreage holds a solid reputation as being an recognized name in the legal marijuana business. Between 2017 and 2019, the company rose to become one of the largest cannabis companies in the US. But the biggest story to hit in recent times is the fact that the company will be acquired by Canopy Growth for a whopping $3.4 billion. This means that Canopy Growth will not only enjoy its home market but easily be able to focus on the US market as well.

13: Trulieve Cannabis

Stock Symbol: TCNNF (OTC Markets Group)

Trulieve is a company that likes to avoid risking too much. As we discussed earlier, the American cannabis product manufacturer focuses on its home base of Florida. This has ensured that the company constantly projects growth, since the Florida market is a large one.

14: AbbVie

Stock Symbol: ABBV (OTC Markets Group)

Similar to GW Pharmaceuticals, AbbVie does not directly deal with cannabis products. However, its most popular product is a drug infused with cannabidiol, Marinol. The drug has been approved by the U.S. Food and Drug Administration. Marinol is used to relieve vomiting and nausea in patients who are undergoing chemotherapy. It's link to cancer treatment has given it a big boost in profits.

14: Medicine Man Technologies

Stock Symbol: MDCL (OTC Markets Group)

One of the lesser known companies is Medicine Man Technologies. The company does not deal with cannabis products or products infused with cannabidiol. Rather, it focuses on the legal aspects of setting up a cannabis firm or retail setup. From application support to licensing, Medicine Man Technologies provides a plethora of assistance to those who would like to start their business in the cannabis industry. With the number of legalization laws that will be going out this year, investors are optimistic that Medicine Man Technologies will soon have a lot of business and companies seeking its consultancy services.

Chapter 5: Considerations before Investing in Marijuana Stocks

You might suddenly feel confident about pot stocks. But your work is not over yet. There are still a few questions you have to ask yourself before you begin your investment, namely the ones mentioned below.

Question 1: Are Marijuana Stocks Showing Any Potential?

Most analysts believe that the cannabis industry is set to grow by up to 35% within the next five years. The fact is that many countries in the world are now focused on marijuana legalization procedures, and market research experts have also predicted huge growth in the industry.

However, there are still skeptics who predict that the industry will take a dip in the coming months.

This is not something that is unique to the pot industry. Even major tech giants such as Apple have skeptics who believe that the stocks will take a dip for the worse. You should treat every marijuana stock like any other stock. Understand the company and market before making your decision.

Question 2: Is There Legal Support for Marijuana?

The answer to this question depends on the region or area you reside in. I highly recommend that you don't base your decisions on assumptions. Check the latest marijuana laws in your state and act accordingly.

Question 3: Is the Public Supportive of the Legalization of Cannabis?

According to CBS News (Williams, 2017), the support for marijuana has grown tremendously over recent years, with the majority of American adults in favor of cannabis legalization.

Question 4: Are Marijuana Companies Taxed?

They are, but their tax procedures are a bit different from other companies. The American government takes a cut of the profits and excludes the cost of goods sold. This means that the company has to pay taxes based on its gross profit. Currently, this is not a norm and is a procedure that is unique to cannabis companies.

This reduces profit margins of the companies, and the government gets to take as much as possible from them.

Question 5: Can Anyone Export Marijuana?

Currently, there are restrictions on marijuana exports. Unless the company has been provided explicit permission from the government, it can only focus on distributing to local markets. However, with new legalization laws coming up, things will change for many cannabis businesses.

Question 6: Why Hasn't the U.S. Government Legalized Marijuana Yet?

This is a fairly complex question that does not provide any easy answers. Currently, the government is focused more on healthcare and tax reforms to pay much attention to cannabis reforms. Additionally, policymakers still believe that they don't have enough evidence to make an informed decision. However, the Farm Bill is a step in the right direction. With many states showing just how profitable marijuana business can be and science producing new and insightful research into marijuana, it won't be long before the government takes note.

Question 7: Is Investing Options Limited to Canada and U.S.?

Absolutely not. As we discussed before, other countries are also legalizing marijuana, and many have given the green light for the use of cannabis in the medical sector. Keep an eye out on the countries mentioned in this book.

Question 8: If the Marijuana Industry is Young, Is It Wise to Invest Now?

Typically, when an industry is young, it is prone to numerous fluctuations. However, the worst of the fluctuations seem to have already occurred. As expansion is the next plan for many companies, you might be able to see growth in various areas of the cannabis industry.

Question 9: Without Banks and Venture Capitalists, How Are Marijuana Companies Able to Fund Themselves?

While there are no financial institutions or VCs showing their support for the cannabis industry yet, many companies receive high levels of capital influx from their investors. Because the sentiment surrounding cannabis companies is quite positive, companies do not have trouble securing investments. Furthermore, bigger companies are looking to take over numerous cannabis companies, which is the case with

Canopy Growth being taken over by Constellation Brands.

Question 10: Is Investing in Marijuana Stocks a Wise Decision?

It is important to understand that despite the growing optimism surrounding cannabis stocks, they are still stocks. They function like any other market security. This means that you should be prepared to tolerate some amount of risk. If you feel uncomfortable taking chances, then try to conduct market research on your own about the stocks you are interested in. Become well-versed about the stock, and when you are comfortable, you can consider investing.

Myths About Cannabis Industry

Recently, there have been some myths cropping up in the minds of the public, either due to misinformation or a lack of awareness of the full picture. But what are these myths? Let us explore them and find out if there is any truth to these claims. Spoiler: there isn't.

Myth #1: The Medicinal Cannabis Market in Canada Is On a Decline

Because of the spread of recreational marijuana in Canada, many people have wrongly assumed that the medicinal cannabis sector is going to take a dive into loss territory. That is not true.

In fact, new research into the benefits of cannabis has increased its demand in the medical community. Furthermore, the Canadian government has started providing financial incentives to people who purchase medicinal marijuana from within the country. While it is true that the recreational market is much larger, it does not automatically indicate a poor performance for medical cannabis.

Myth #2: There Is Going to Be a Problem with Supply in the Near Future

On the contrary, with the number of countries that are jumping on the "legalize marijuana" bandwagon, things are poised to get better for marijuana supply chains. The global cannabis market is going to be far larger than Canada or the U.S., and to take advantage of it, there has to be a proper supply network.

Myth #3: Retail Cannabis Is Experiencing a Sluggish Growth

If you look at the retail landscape, then you will notice that more and more cannabis outlets are appearing all over the country, and even across the globe. The consumer cannabis market is bigger than ever before.

Retail marijuana market had already increased its performance by 35% in 2018 and showed a $12 billion revenue by the end of 2019 (McVay, 2019).

Myth #4: The Marijuana Market Is Only Split into the Medicinal and Recreation Categories

The presence of this myth is understandable. Many investors and experts mention only two marijuana markets; that they often forget there is a third market slowly making its presence known to the public. This market is the wellness market. Companies are already manufacturing cannabidiol wellness oils and products.

Myth #5: The Global Marijuana Market Is Not Well Set-up

While the laws concerning marijuana are taking time to see the light of day, there are many established companies that are already distributing on a global scale. Simply check more details about the company you would like to invest in to get more details of their international business.

Ethical Concerns in the Marijuana Industry

Anyone who is planning to invest in the cannabis industry is already aware that there are some ethical concerns surrounding it.

Opponents of marijuana legalization often bring to light the fact that consuming cannabis leads to a loss of control of a person's personality and identity, thus making him or her harmful to self and to others. Proponents of the legalization procedures like to point out that even alcohol causes a loss of self, leading to dangerous situations. In fact, according to the National Highway Traffic Safety Administration, one person dies in a drunk-driving related accident every 50 minutes. That amounts to nearly 30 accidents a day. The message that is often spread among people who consume alcohol is to drink responsibly and make sure that they are not driving under the influence. Legalization supporters believe in the same message of consuming marijuana responsibly. Furthermore, research has shown that alcohol causes more damage to the brain than marijuana (Medical News Today, n.d.).

Another problem that opponents of legalization like to bring up is that allowing marijuana distribution increases the crime rate in an area or state. However, this claim has also been debunked. U.S. states that border Mexico include a high number of drug cartels. You might think that the legalization procedures are exactly what the cartels are looking for.

However, the surprising result of the legalization process is that people have official sources to purchase marijuana. This has caused drug cartels to lose a large portion of their business to regulated cannabis outlets (Doward, 2018). In other words, legalization has decreased illegal distribution. This situation has even caused violent crime to drop by nearly 13% since the fewer illegal distributors on the street, the lower the chances of a violent incident.

While there are ethical concerns surrounding the legalization of marijuana, you will find that the move to legalize has shown more benefits than issues.

Chapter 6:
Getting Started with Pot Stocks

Ready to get started on trading with marijuana stocks? Here is a guide to get you going in the right direction.

A Step-by-Step Guide to Buying Marijuana Stocks

Step #1: Brokerage Account

The first thing you will require even before you start exploring marijuana stocks is a brokerage account. I am going to list some of the best brokers you can use for trading further into this chapter.

It typically takes less than 15 minutes to open an account. Make sure that you are comfortable with the features and services offered by the broker before signing up for their services. Check out the commission structure of the broker and make sure that it is comfortable to you. Do note that brokers with more features usually ask for a slightly higher commission. You have to choose how to balance features versus price.

Step #2: Assess the Market

Before you can even think of investing, you need to check the market. Use sources such as *Yahoo! Finance, The Motley Fool, The Wall Street Journal*, and *Bloomberg*, among many other services, to find your company. Then look at the latest news and updates about the stock. Look at historical performance. Make sure that you don't jump to conclusions. For example, just because you notice one instance of a dip in share prices, it does not automatically mean that the stock is not worth your investment. You should also be looking at the latest news in the industry and the overall market.

Step #3: Make Your Purchase

When you have decided on the stock you would like to buy, you should then look at the difference between what buyers are willing to pay for the stock and sellers are comfortable accepting. This difference is known as the bid spread. When the bid spread is large, then it is usually an indication of thinly traded stocks. In other words, when the trading volume of the stock is small, or "thin," then the bid spread becomes bigger. Another reason for the wide bid spread is the volatility in the market.

Remember that just because there is a smaller trade volume, it does not mean that the company is performing poorly. Smaller companies have fewer investors than larger companies. When looking at smaller companies, you should examine their past performance, future goals and plans, market conditions, and legal developments.

When you have reviewed your purchase, hit the "buy" button. With that, you are good to go.

Step #4: Keep an Eye Out for Your Stocks

Do not purchase more than you can handle. Most brokers don't place a minimum amount for investment. You can get started with as low as $1. However, the bigger question is: how much should you invest?

How much you invest depends on how much risk you can bear. Try to think of your investment in terms of a loss. If you were to invest a certain amount into a stock and lose that money, would it disrupt your life? Will it force you to make sacrifices with your finances? If so, then you are taking more risk than you can handle.

You can also set aside a certain amount for your investment. Once done, invest 10% of it initially. For example, if you are ready to put in $1,000 into a stock, don't use the entire amount you have as investment. Use $100, and then examine the market. If you feel optimistic, then invest $100 more. This allows you to strategize better and keep your investments within your allotted budget.

Bonus Step: Don't Borrow

Don't get into the temptation of borrowing money from any source. If you lose more money, then you might find yourself in a difficult situation. No investor had ever made it big instantly. They had to experiment and learn the market. You should be doing the same, learning and experimenting with the market.

The Best Brokerage Company

Having a brokerage company is useful because they provide a sense of reliability. You need to know where your money is going. A brokerage company will be able to keep track of transactions and the results of your investment. Moreover, brokers have a vast experience of the market and some of them even offer consultancy services.

Ally Invest

If you are a price-conscious investor or a beginner, then Ally Invest might be right for you. You will be provided with easy-to-use tools and a vast repository of information and research. They also have very low trading commissions, and they don't require a minimum amount to open an account.

AvaTrade

AvaTrade offers a wide variety of instruments to trade with. But one of its standout features is the social trading features that allows you to interact with other investors. There is also a rich collection of research materials for you to make use of.

Merrill Edge

For casual investors, Merrill Edge is the ideal broker. Not only does it provide a host of tools, but it is also linked to Bank of America, allowing integration between the platform and bank customers. Even if you are not a customer of Bank of America, the broker provides many options to help with your investments.

Interactive Brokers

For active traders, Interactive Brokers is a good choice for investments. It's commission margins, while not as low as Ally Invest, is still in the low end of the range when you compare it to other brokers. The platform allows you to trade in 120 markets across 31 countries. This makes it easier for you to find a particular stock.

Tradestation

This broker has a long track record, making it a trusted tool among many investors. It also has a greater degree of transparency than other brokers. Do note that the platform may not suit a casual investor, even though it has tried to create features for casual investors.

10 Ways to Master the Market

Tip #1

Keep updating yourself with the latest news about your stock, and the cannabis industry in general. Use online news sources to find out as much information as you can. You need to have the right knowledge to make informed decisions. Often, you might find useful trading tips.

Tip #2

Read books. Receiving investment tips from professionals will help you understand the market and how to invest wisely.

Tip #3

Use a demo trading account to practice your strategy. Using a live account might be risky. Try to get comfortable with trading by practicing on a demo account.

Tip #4

You can also buy an online trading course. Make sure that you choose from reputable sources. There are many courses that are very affordable.

Tip #5

Make use of free chart platforms. They will help you get financial information about the company. Usually, charts will be provided by your broker, but it is always good to get as many details as possible from other sources.

Tip #6

If there is a trade seminar near you, try to attend it. There is a wealth of information you can glean from such seminars and can form valuable connections.

Tip #7

Don't be afraid to emulate the strategies of successful traders. If something is already working well, then perhaps it can repeat its success with you as well.

Tip #8

Make use of social trading features, if your broker has them. Exchanging information with other traders is a good way to find out more about a stock and what other traders are planning.

Tip #9

Head over to YouTube. There are many trading videos and tutorials that you can use. There are even beginner courses that will help you get started.

Tip #10

Invest in ETFs. I have already provided you with a list of ETFs to work with. Discover the latest information about those ETFs so that you are able to make better investment decisions.

Chapter 7:
Common Investment
Mistakes You Should Avoid

It happens to everyone; one minute they are looking at their stock rise, feeling confident about their strategy, and suddenly, something happens that completely shifts their perspective. It helps if you are aware of these common mistakes that many investors, even veterans, make.

Mistake #1: Lack of Understanding the Investment

Never invest in something you don't understand. You might end up with a much bigger risk than you can understand. Use the tips provided in the previous chapter to better understand your investments before you think of making a move on it.

Mistake #2: Getting Emotionally Invested in a Company

When people see the company they invested in doing well, they become emotionally invested in that company. That way, even if the company starts showing poor performance, they continue to invest in it, not because they have a plan in mind but because they liked how the company performed previously.

Always use information to your benefit. If you think that a company is not doing well, stop and reconsider your strategy. Or choose another company.

Mistake #3: Lack of Patience

You are not going to get a huge return within a short period of time. Investment is a slow and steady progress game. Don't worry about what the movie with the brilliant mathematician or hacker tells you; reality does not play out that way. In real life, you need to be disciplined and focused.

Mistake #4: High Investment Turnover

A turnover occurs when you jump in and out of an investment. When you start doing it too many times, then you won't give each stock time to mature. You are going to miss out on long-term benefits and might even end up making a loss quickly.

Mistake #5: Getting Obsessed with Market Timing

It is not easy to successfully time the market because of its unpredictability. Even investors who have decades of experience never try to time the market because their experience has taught them that such tacts rarely work. You need to focus on allocating your resources and gathering information.

Mistake #6: Waiting Too Long

Some investors wait too long to invest, always thinking that the best opportunity is about to arrive. But rarely does such a "best opportunity" appear. If you do not feel like taking a huge risk, then always start small. Get used to the market before you think of betting big.

Mistake #7: Buying and Selling Using Emotions

Don't buy or sell because you have a "good feeling" about it. Use information to your advantage. Make informed decisions and refer to various sources before you finalize your decision. Without due diligence, you are going to increase risk, even when your position is not that risky.

Mistake #8: Don't Think about Beating the Market

It might sound good to say that you have "beaten the market" and made a good profit out of it. But in reality, success does not occur because you beat the market. You should keep a set of goals that you would lie to achieve. These goals will help you define your strategy and help you decide how long you would like to trade with a particular security.

Mistake #9: Having Unrealistic Expectations

Let's face it. Everyone wants to strike gold when they start investing. But it helps to manage your expectations. Stocks involve risk. They can change directions suddenly, and if you have been thinking of winning big, then you might be in for a huge disappointment. Keep your mind focused on the trade and your research process. Don't worry about the end result too soon.

Conclusion

The world of marijuana trading is still in its infancy.

However, one cannot deny the potential the industry has. The cannabis industry is an exciting one. Even with all the restrictions that exist today, the industry is heading for growth. When the restrictions are finally removed, that growth is going to be explosive.

You might already notice many cannabis products released under a brand name. The fact that marijuana companies are spending more on marketing and branding efforts shows just how much growth potential the industry has, especially considering that the legalization process occurred in 2018.

It is not just the recreational sector of the cannabis industry that is going to show growth. With science showing more and more benefits of cannabis, the medicinal products using cannabis is going to rise as well. The benefits of cannabis can be seen on both mental and physical ailments. That alone can make it a hot commodity in the coming years. There are already a variety of products that use cannabidiol and hemp. Soon, numerous drugs using cannabis components might become common in the market.

Let's not forget the fact that many countries around the world are working to legalize marijuana. If that happens, the growth is going to be staggering. Much of the present growth predictions are based on the current political and legal positions. If things develop for the better, then those predictions are going to change for the better.

One thing is for certain: marijuana stocks are on a course to go high.

Alexander Bercovich

References

BDS Analytics. (2019). *The State of Legal Cannabis Markets – 7th Edition*. Arcview Market Research.

Daniller, A. (2019). Two-thirds of Americans support marijuana legalization. Retrieved 28 February 2020, from https://www.pewresearch.org/fact-tank/2019/11/14/americans-support-marijuana-legalization

Dorbian, I. (2019). New Cannabis Report Predicts Legal Sales To Reach Nearly $30 Billion By 2025. Retrieved 26 February 2020, from https://www.forbes.com/sites/irisdorbian/2019/09/24/new-cannabis-report-predicts-legal-sales-to-reach-nearly-30-billion-by-2025/#33621c7d1121

Evans, P. (2019). 8 incredible facts about the booming US marijuana industry. Retrieved 26 February 2020, from https://www.businessinsider.sg/weed-us-marijuana-industry-facts-2019-5?r=US&IR=T

Geiger, A., & Gramlich, J. (2019). 6 facts about marijuana. Retrieved 26 February 2020, from https://www.pewresearch.org/fact-tank/2019/11/22/facts-about-marijuana/

Grinspoon, P. (2018). Medical marijuana - Harvard Health Blog. Retrieved 27 February 2020, from https://www.health.harvard.edu/blog/medical-marijuana-2018011513085

Williams, S. (2017). Support for Legalizing Marijuana Hits Another Record High, National Survey Shows. Retrieved 28 February 2020, from https://www.fool.com/investing/2017/10/29/support-for-legalizing-marijuana-hits-another-reco.aspx

Williams, S. (2020). Why the Coronavirus Is Bad News for Pot Stocks | The Motley Fool. Retrieved 27 February 2020, from https://www.fool.com/investing/2020/02/11/why-the-coronavirus-is-bad-news-for-pot-stocks.aspx